FH4

CW00796362

Written By ©Cindy

Published By Marian Bonelli

PublishedByMe.blogspot.com

ISBN-13 978-1985407992

ISBN-10 198540799X

Note from the Publisher:

Cindy and I met on a bus in Wales, the replacement for a train cancellation; we got to talking and I heard she was writing about her life as a child and through young adulthood.

Cindy got working towards writing more down, and remembering a past she had put out of her mind; some of which for good reason.

I hope she has found some answers and some peace in working through her thoughts and memories; and in her own words, putting them into print.

She deserves congratulations; it is not always an easy thing to do.

Marian @publishedbyme.com

Dedication:

I dedicate this book to the memory of Pat and her mum who lived next door to me when I was a child.

And to thank all my friends I have had over the years.

Also my family,
I would not be here today if it was not for them.

Cindy

Note from the author:

I have always wanted to write a book about my life. I had a very bad beginning and it helps to write things down, it has been a very long journey with a lot of ups and downs but I got there in the end.

This is my story...

It is the year 1937.
Gladys and Fred's wedding day, they had a very good day.

But all too soon Fred had to go back to the war, Gladys missed him. In her next letter to him Gladys told him she was having a baby. When he came home she said you have a son. They called him Don. The years went by then they had Geoff. Then war was over and Fred came home for good. They were good days.

It was coming up to Christmas, Gladys and Fred have got a new home and Fred has a new job on the railway as a porter, things are looking up and they all had a good Christmas.

In the new year Gladys was not very well, then she found out she was having a baby, she did not have a good pregnancy and was in and out of hospital. Don at that time was ten, and did a lot for Fred and Geoff, so that his dad could be with his mum. He was of great help, and in time Gladys went into hospital to have the baby, they called me Cynthia; but Mum was still very ill, and it was a difficult time for them.

By the time Christmas came along, things were better, and it was a good time, Dad was doing well in his new job, so they all had lots of new things and Mum was much better.

The next year also was a good one, we all went to the seaside, they were happy days indeed.

But they were also the end of happy days for a long time; Mum became very ill again, and remained so for the next two years. Don helped out as before and did a lot for Dad, Geoff and myself.

Sadly Mum passed away when I was just two, Don twelve and Geoff six.

Dad had a lady to look after me and the house, while Dad continued to work very hard; we had happy days out at the seaside.

One day Dad came home, and there was a man at the door from the council, because the lady had not paid the rent we were evicted. I went to a nursery initially and Geoff and Don into a home. Then Geoff and I had to go into a home together, it was called Fairhaven. This must have been a very hard time for Dad, he came to see us as much as he could, but I could not understand why he had to go away, I missed him and could not remember Mum very much; I did not know where Don was.

One day Dad came to see us with a lady, her name was Mary; he said she is going to be your new mum, and it wasn't long after that they came to take the two of us to our new home; it was at the top of a hill and across the road were many streets, the houses all had lanes running behind them. Mary loved our dad a great deal but she was never very loving to me or Geoff. I couldn't bring myself to call her mum; she was very hard and could not give me any affection. It was good to be with Dad, and with Geoff, but he was hardly ever in.

Dad got a job at the railway station and was happy that we were sharing a home once more. Don never lived with us but did come to visit. One day he came in his new car, he took Dad and I out for the day.

Dad and Mary never fell out and I think they were happy. Geoff was always going out and I wanted to go with him, but he always said no. So quite often I would go across the road to see new friends Susan and Pat. We would go down to the station to see Dad; their mum and dad were very nice we would go out a lot together, and when Dad had a day off work we would all go out for the day to see Mary's mum and sister. I loved going to Clent we always had fun and if Mary was with Dad she was all right.

When Dad came home from work he would give me some of his tips, we would count it to see how much he had got, and go across the road to where there was a shop, it was at the top of a man's garden. In time he opened a new shop at the top of the road, he was very nice, and everyone went to his shop before we went to school.

I loved going to school we had lots of fun, and Dad would ask me if I had had a good time.

I will never forget the day I had my bike, Susan had one too, in time we all had one. Susan and I were out all the time on our bikes.

I know I did not have a lot of love from Mary, but Dad did love both Geoff and I a great deal, and Mary was happy with Dad.

Don is coming today, we are going to the park, it is across the road from the railway station, it is very big, it has a bandstand we have a picnic and listen to the music and see Dad if he is at work.

I love going to the park, if it was Dad's day off, Dad Mary and I would go for the day.

We are all going to see Gran at Clent, and Mary's Sister Olive. I love going to Clent, Aunt Olive was always very good to me, and also I loved the horses. I spent a lot of time with them, they were Aunt Olive's horses, she let me take them up the hill, it was the best time. I was very happy in the countryside, I never wanted to go home.

Gran is at work today, I am going too, Gran worked at a school doing the cleaning I would go too with my dustpan. I would love to go to her school, but I would miss Dad, it is time to go home. Happy days, I will miss them.

Don came today it is always good to see him, we are going to town then to the railway station to see Dad, I love going to the station to see the trains, there was always lots going on and things to do.

It is my first day at school, it is not far away, the first time the bell went I went home; then when I went back the next day the teacher wanted to know where I had gone the day before? I had not been time to go home. After that Mary never took me to school again, but everyone was always kind to me there.

One day I was especially looking forward to going to school. Dad was at work all weekend, and Mary was not happy.

I was late, and had fallen over, I had hurt my leg, it had a bad cut and my teacher was looking after me, they had asked what had happened, I told them a man had knocked me over and I was very upset.

But it was not true, I made it up, it was so good that everyone was looking after me. The police came, and Dad. No one found out, not even Dad, and that was the beginning of me having a world of my own. If I was not happy I would go into my world, and tell my friends that I was okay.

When Dad was at home we had good times; we would go to the seaside for the day, or I can go to the railway station where Dad's pals were nice to me, always happy days.

Don fell out with Mary I do not see much of him anymore.

When there is no one else in the house, and it's just me, Mary is not nice; I do not think she loves me I never get a hug or kiss, no affection at all. Today Mary is not happy, I do not know why she is very upset, Mary was only happy if Dad was there. She just did not love me or want me around and in time things got bad, she would hit me. I was scared of her but if Dad was there she was all right, he just did not know how bad it was, no one did.

I am going to a new school soon, my next door neighbour was very nice, her daughter Pat went to school with me, all the mums were good to me and I had many new friends.

Mary got a new job at the hospital, it was good, I did not see a lot of her. I had more time with Dad and Don happy days. I would meet Dad from work and push his bike up the hill, we all had a bike and went out often.

It is Christmas, Dad will be home for three days I am so happy, it is Christmas morning even Mary is nice we all had a very happy day.

One day when Dad was at work and Geoff was out, as always Mary was not nice to me, she did not want me, she said I was bad and would hit me. Why did she not love me, if Dad was around she was all right, Dad did not know how unhappy I was, I did not want to upset her.

It is the school holidays, I had been out with Pat; Dad and Mary were at work, when I got home Don is there looking very sad, Dad has been hurt at work, we are going to the hospital, they will not let me see him, Don took me home, we went back the next day but Dad had passed away, what will I do now, things will never be the same again.

When Dad passed away I never said goodbye to him or tell him 'I love you and I will never forget you.' I still go down to the railway station, my dad's friends are always there to give me love, I also have Don, Geoff is never home.

I did not get to say goodbye to Dad the day of the funeral either, they sent me to the shop and when I came back they had gone, there was just me sitting on the step I was very sad. I will never forget him, also it was my birthday I was 12, I will never forget that day.

Not long after I lost Dad Mary took me to Edinburgh, Scotland, for a week. Just me and her, we went to the castle and the parks, we did have a good time, but when we got back she was not good, I do not understand after that how Mary went so very bad.

I was glad to go back to school, Geoff was never in so he did not know what was going on, no one did.

When I came home from school Mary would say why are you not dead, she just wanted my dad, there was a belt on the back of the door she would hit me with it.

Pat's mum next door was very good, she would give me jam butties and pop, and a bag of chips.

When Mary went back to work things were very bad. She would lock me out all day, I would sit in the outside toilet before I went to school, I did not have nice things, at school they made fun of me. She did not give me anything to eat, I had no dinner at school, and Pat's mum gave me my tea.

One day when I came home Mary had locks put on all the cupboards and doors even my bedroom.

I do miss Dad and cannot understand why she doesn't love me, all I ever wanted was to be loved and wanted.

One day Don gave me some nice things to go to school in. I have left them next door, Mary does not know that I have them. I hope now they will not make fun of me.

One day Mary was in a very bad mood, it was a Sunday. Pat was out with her mum I was in my room when she locked it. I was left there for two days.

After that I did not want to go home, I never knew what she would do next.

I was very frightened of Mary, at school I would tell them all that I had good times and that I was happy, if they had had a good weekend so did I; only Pat knew that was not true.

In my bedroom I had a picture my dad gave me, he told me always to keep it, I also had little things Dad had given me over the years. I keep them under the floorboards so Mary could not see them. I do not know what happened to them, I would love to get them back one day.

Today Mary has come home to find me next door having fun. That was it, I had to go home she would not stop hitting me.

I was so frightened she kept saying why are you not dead. I do not want you or love you, then she locked me in my bedroom. I do not know how long I was in there, I miss my dad, and Don too, even Don did not know all that went on.

Today a lady came to see me, she was asking me if I was happy at home with Mary and if I was locked out all day when Mary was at work, it was hard answering her with Mary sitting there, Mary told her that she did not want me and to take me into a home. Not long after I went from school to a court it was not nice.

That day from school I was very scared in court, I had to tell them all that she had done to me and said, she said I was making it all up.

In the end there was just me in a room telling them what was going on. Pat and her mum from next door came too, they told the court how she locked me out of her home when she was at work, and that I had to sit in the toilet outside until she came back, they also told the court that she hits me with a belt and did not want me, and that I did not have any food, I was always hungry.

Mary told the court that she had taken me to the mental health department saying she did not want me and to be taken into

care, they said I was in need of care and protection, and I woul
stay until I was eighteen in the care of the county council. Whe
it was all over she said she was going to kill me.

I was very scared; they took me back into the room where I wa
before. Don came, I was very upset, he said you will be all righ
now, then he had to go, I worried what will happen now. Afte
the court case a lady came to see me, her name was Miss J
she was always there for me, I cannot see anyone. I went to a
home called The Laurels, they took my school bag and askec
me to take my clothes off and get in the bath. I was so scared
They gave me some of their clothes. I did not see my schoo.
bag again, I did not know what happened to Mary. I knew no
one and I cannot go home for any of my things, or go to see
Pat, I did not have a lot, but what I did have they took it from
me, and they gave me a number, 4.

I do miss my dad I am always thinking of him.

A lady and man came today they said we are your Aunt Kate
and Uncle Henry, I found out that Mary said they were not
allowed to visit when she married my dad, I was so happy I
have got an aunt and uncle and hope they can give me a home.
I have now been for the weekend to Henry and Kate's, I do not
think that I can stay there, they have not got any children, and
do not know what to do with me it is very sad.

The matron at the home said that I cannot go back to Stafford
because Mary was not happy and would hurt me. I am sad
today thinking of Aunt Kate and Uncle Henry, I miss all the
years I did not have with them, I could have been happier with
them. Why did Dad not let me see them? If I had, as they did
not have children of their own, then maybe they could have
taken me, why did they not have me.

I was only there a week and I was transferred, Miss J. said I am
going to take you to Dawlish, a home by the sea, it is on top of a
hill, High House. I was very nervous, I did not know anyone, I
miss Don, and Pat from next door. It is not bad here, it is a very

big house, I am so lost I do not know what to do, and I still have my number 4.

It is Monday and I have got to go to school, it was mixed boys and girls, lots of boys. I was not happy and Miss J. came to see me a lot here. I had to face that I did not have a mum and dad and live in a home. I cannot tell them at school that I am happy and have a good home, nor can I go away for the weekends, because they knew I came from the home up the hill.

Miss J. came to see me on Saturdays to see how my week went at school, it was hard, I had to be me, and remember all that had happened to me. I was happier in my own world, no one can hurt me and I have my mum and dad.

Remembering all the bad things was very hard. I would sit in the window looking at the sea and wish it would all go away, I just did not know what to do, I was very sad, will I ever be happy again? It will be Christmas soon and I am not looking forward to it, the girls and boys in the home are nice to me, on Sundays we all go out for the day, there are twenty of us. There was one girl Sue, we became good pals, she was in my class at school, we had good times.

Christmas was not too bad I had a lot of nice things, but I did miss Dad and Don.

This Saturday was not a good one, I was remembering when Mary would lock me in my bedroom for days, I was so scared. She would let me out at night to go to the toilet and then I had to go back. I sometimes wish I can go to sleep and not wake up, I would then be with my mum and dad. But instead I would wake up and have to face the day and go to school.

Miss J. would say it is good to remember the things Mary did, but for me it hurts too much, and I did not want to.

Today Miss J. was asking what was Mary saying to you? Mary was not nice when I came home from school, she would hit me, then say that I was not wanted, why are you not dead instead o Dad? Sometimes I did wish that Dad was here, and we were fa away. To me Dad was with me all the time. Miss J. was saying have got to let go of Dad and face up to the fact that he is no coming back.

Bit by bit things are getting better with Miss J. being there fo me, it has been a very hard year.

I know now that Mary will never hurt me again, I will never go back to her.

Miss J. came to see me today, she was saying that soon we will all be leaving High House and going to new homes. No one was going with me.

It is my last day at school, I will miss them, I did have happy times with them. I had a fab day and I will never forget them, but I cannot stay at Dawlish.

It is my last Saturday with Miss J. at High House. You are going to Fairhaven she was saying, you have been there before, it was when Dad was evicted for not paying the rent. I was 4 at the time; it was then also that I had been given my number.

I know you will be happy, it will be a new start for you, you will go to work. I just know you will be all right. Miss J. gave me nametags, FH No.4, for my things, I did not have a lot.

All too soon I was going; we are all at the railway station to say goodbye, and this time it was only me who was going to a new home. But I had been there before, and I am better now and looking forward to going to Fairhaven. I was nervous but happy, a new beginning and there was a lot to look forward to getting, a job and new friends.

The matron of Fairhaven would always say to us "I know all that you do, I do not miss anything!" It was very hard, you did not have a lot, even your personal things were given to the other kids, and everything else had your number on it. All I had were three bras, six pairs of knickers, two pyjamas and three waist slips.

For work	For Best
1 mac	1 coat
1pr slacks	1 pinafore dress
2 skirts	1 jumper
1pr shoes	1 blouse
1pr boots	1 pr shoes

Our best was only for Sunday's to go to church, or going to the youth club. At Fairhaven if we were not happy we would sing 'We have got to get out of here, if it is the last thing we do.' It became our song at Fairhaven. The last weekend in the month was visiting time, sometimes Don and Pat came, but a lot of the time no one came. Sometimes I went to town for the day it was better than staying at home and no one coming to see me.

When I was sent to Fairhaven from Dawlish I did not know anyone, but soon I had a lot of new friends. There were thirty of us; I would look after the little ones, they did not stay long before they went home.

We all had jobs to do, and would get money on a Saturday I never had any from Mary.

Today I went to Stewarts & Sons limited for a job. I got it I will be working Monday to Friday 8am to 5:30pm. It was good there, I did a lot of things with the glass, I would paint designs on them and everyone was good to me.

When I got home to Fairhaven I still had my jobs to do, it was hard.

On a Saturday we would look to see what jobs we were doing for the week, the list was on the back of the kitchen door then in the afternoon we had our pocket money. I had to give my wages to the uncle I cannot open it, I got 10 shillings back.

I am going out with Janet she is nice and has looked after me we share a bedroom with Helen and Sandra; we are all good friends there is also John, Jimmy and David, we all go around together.

On Sundays we have to go to church, I am happy here. No one is hitting me or locking me out and I have nice things, but I miss Dad and Don, I hope Don will come and see me soon.

Today I went to the youth club I had a very good time I met Bill he was good at dancing and I love it too. I went every week it was something to look forward to and I made lots of new friends there. Bill asked me out to the pictures, he had to ask the uncle at the home, the uncle went to Bill's mum and dad to meet them.

As time went on I saw a lot of Bill, I went to meet his mum and dad and sister. They were all very kind to me. On a Sunday I would go for my tea, it was good to be part of them all. I wish I can stay with them; Bill and I did go out a lot with his sister, I loved going to the youth club.

One day at work a girl called Janet was not nice to me, she said she was glad she was not in the home up the road and that she had a good home, in the end I hit her, she told her dad he came to work, my boss went to see the uncle at the home, what will I do now? But it did not go to court, and my boss said it wasn't my fault, that she had asked for it, Janet lost her job but I did not, I do love my job, they were all very kind to me.

It is Saturday and me Bill and Barbara his sister, are going to see a band at the town hall, I am staying at Bill's house I am so happy. I did not think I could be this happy again. It was a very happy year going to see the bands and staying with Bills family.

I am going to Clent for the weekend to see my Gran and Aunt Olive, I did hope that I can go and stay with them when I came out of the home, but Gran is too old and Aunt Olive is going away. All too soon it was time to go back to the home, and sadly I never saw Gran and Aunt Olive again.

Today we are all going to Dawlish for two weeks; I do not want to go. I asked the uncle and Aunt Ann, if I can stay with Bill and his mum and dad. Aunt Ann looked after us all in the home also Uncle John. When I was at Fairhaven Aunt Ann would teach me how to cook, clean shoes, and do the ironing, and to look nice when I went out to the youth club. If we went to see a band at the town hall Aunt Ann came too, if we were going to be late home, when we were out I never called her Aunt Ann, just Ann.

Uncle John said it will be a good holiday I will have fun at the seaside, but to me I will remember bad times, I do not want to think of those days.

Helen, Janet, Sandra, John and Jimmy are my best pals in the home, and they all looked after me when we got to Dawlish; we did have a lot of happy days we would all go out for the day, I saw a lot of Dawlish. And all too soon it was time to go back to the home, but this time I was happy to go back to Fairhaven.

At work we sat overlooking the river. I was always looking out of the window, there were men fishing, and boats going up and down, there was always something going on.

Today Ken Dodd is coming to see us, we are all very excited. He is very funny; we are all going to see his show.

Christmas is coming, everyone is going home, but I have no one to go home to, I do not know where Geoff is, and I hope to see Don after the new year, I have not seen him for a long time and I miss him.

It is Christmas morning there is only me and Aunt Ann in this big house, and I wonder why did they not let me go to Bill's? Christmas is not a happy time for me, I remember the good times with Dad, Don and Geoff. It is Boxing Day, and Aunt Ann said I can go to Bill's for tea. When I got there his sister and mum and dad gave me lots of hugs and good food. I had a very good time, I did not want to go back, it was good to be part of family.

Today Don is coming to see me, I was hoping to go and stay with him for the weekend, but he had a lady with him, he said he was going to get married to her, we had a good day I am happy the uncle said I can go to the wedding, her name is Pat, her mum and dad are very nice.

Today I am going to Stafford for Don and Pat's wedding I will be staying at Pat's mum and dad's house, Mary and Colin, this Mary is okay! I had a good time but all too soon had to go back to Fairhaven and also to work.

Work is okay, I look forward to Friday when I get paid, but the 10 Shillings has to last me the week. I had fun at the weekend Bill and I went to the town hall to meet his sister, sometimes Helen and Janet would come too, there was always a good band on and we would dance all night. On the way home we went to the fish and chip shop, there was a man in the shop who had nowhere to go and not a lot to eat, we said 'come with us to the home,' when they have all gone to bed we will let you in, his name was Sam.

We all looked after Sam for a long time, then one day he got a job and a new home. The uncle and matron never did know about him; matron had said she knew everything that went on, but she didn't really know all of what we got up to. She never did know about Sam! I hope he is all right, I never saw him again after Fairhaven.

Today is my birthday I will be 16 years old, I am thinking of Dad and missing him. Don and Pat are coming on Sunday to see me and I am going to Bill's for my birthday; his mum is so good to me I never want to go back. I also had a good day at work today, I had a birthday cake, I'd never had one before and some nice presents, it was a very happy day, Bill's present to me was a necklace.

A new girl came today her name is Sue and we became good friends, on the weekend if I was not seeing Bill we would go out and have fun, we were always up to something. I had a very happy year, but now it will soon be time for me to leave Fairhaven. Across the road is a hospital, I am hoping to go there and then I can still see Bill and all my friends.

Today I am leaving Stewart's it is sad, I did love working there but I have got to find somewhere to live.

I have got a new job at the hospital, I love it and Sue my best pal has also got a job there! She too has got to find somewhere to live, I will miss them all at Fairhaven but we have got to find somewhere to live when we are eighteen we cannot stay there anymore. It is very sad one by one we are all going away.

The matron at the hospital asked to see me today and she told me that I cannot live in. Where do I go now? The uncle at the home has said I am being transferred to Standon Hall hospital, as a domestic this will be my new home, I do not want to be a domestic but I have to go. I have got two weeks to say goodbye to everyone, for Bill and I it will be very hard, I love his mum and dad and sister, I wish I could stay with them. That was the last time I saw Bill's mum dad and sister, I will miss them I hope it is okay at Standon Hall hospital.

I have just got here and already I'm not happy, my bedroom is very big and just me in it, no one is very nice and the matron is very hard, she is always telling me what to do. I am the only domestic living in and they are a lot older than me. In the sitting room I had to ask where can I sit down, no one wanted me there, I was always in my bedroom, just me, I miss them all at Fairhaven; and Bill, his mum dad and sister.

I was put on the men's ward, I just did not know what to do, matron was always there, I even had to ask her if I can go to the shop on my day off. I got the bus to see Bill as I am missing him a lot, but all too soon I have got to go back, if I am late I get told off by my matron. I wish I was 18 already then I can go and live with Bill. I would see Bill at Stafford, matron did not know. He met me off the bus, we go to the pictures or the park then I had to get back to the hospital.

Today a new patient came he was very nice and we got on very well, his name is Tom. After work I go and see him, we go down to the shop, I am very happy with him, but matron was not and was told not to see him again, but I still did until he went home. miss Tom and I am back to being in my room on my own.

Don and Pat, and Pat's mum, came to see me today. Mary Pat's mum asked me to come and stay with her on my days off she went to see matron and she said yes as long as I am not late getting back.

On my days off I went to stay with Mary it was good to begin with, then she would not let Bill come and see me, and matron said it would be best if I did not see him again, I was very unhappy but I had to do as I was told. I miss Bill and his family a great deal.

I will never forget Bill and his family they gave me lots of love and understanding.

I do think a lot about my friends at Fairhaven and hope that they are happy, and one day hope to see them again, I remember a lot of the good times we all had. Sometimes it was hard, I was the only one with no mum or dad, Don and Pat came to see me but I missed Dad the most.

I also miss them at Stewart's they were very good to me it was hard work, but I was happy... why did I have to go away, why did they not let me stay with Bill and his mum and dad.

Today I am going to stay with Mary for the weekend, I am not happy they wanted me to go and stay with her for good when I am 18, I have to do as they say until I'm twenty-one.

Today is my last day at Standon Hall hospital I am going to live at Mary's. I am not happy, I still miss Bill and I do not know where I'm going to work, I will have to find a new job.

There is a factory called the GEC I got a job there, but this time I did not give my pay packet to anyone, I had it. It was so good, I do like my new job and I have got a new friend her name is Sandra, we go to town and have fun. It is getting harder to live at Mary's she is always asking me 'what are you doing.' I can never get it right and when I get in, it is 'where have you been, who have you been with, you are late'... 'You cannot see Sue for the weekend' I was happier at Fairhaven! I still cannot see Bill; I miss him and his family.

Now that I am 18 I can go back to Stafford, Don and Pat do not live there anymore, when I went in the home Don left, he was not happy in Stafford, too many sad times, I do not know what happened to Geoff.

I am not going to live with Mary for long I hope to have a home of my own one day.

Today I'm going to see Pat and all my friends who looked after me when I was with Mary, it has been six years. I hope they still live there and that they remember me.

I did not want to go past the house, it was too sad remembering what went on in there, so I went the back way. When I got to Susan's house I just hoped she was still there with her Mum. I was very nervous when I knocked on the door, but when it opened it was Susan standing there, she looked me up and down and said I cannot believe it's you! Come in, 'Mum! Mum! It is Cynthia.' They did not know me as Cindy, when I left Standon Hall hospital, I was not happy being Cynthia, so now I am Cindy.

Susan and their mum sat looking at me. 'Is it you Cynthia! It cannot be you, sit down Cynthia, I have got something to tell you... When Pat and her mum went to court that day, they did not know where you went, so they asked Mary, she said you went to Clent to your gran's, and one day there was an accider with a car and it killed you! We all thought that you had passe away. We all got you some flowers, and went to church to sa goodbye.' When I left Susan and her mum that day I was ver sad, how can anyone be that hard. Did Mary think that was th end of me.

I just hope one day I will be happy, and someone will love m and give me a home.

I'm looking forward to the weekend, Sandra from the GEC and are going to the fair it is in town for a week. We had lots of fur and met some nice lads, I did not want to go back home I was just not happy staying with Mary. So when the fair left town Sandra and I went with them! We had the best time ever, it was so good, no one telling me what to do and asking me where have you been, we went to lots of places, but in time I had to go back home, I missed my friends. When I went home Sandra came to, I did not go back to Mary's. Sandra and I got a caravan, it was so good to have a home that was mine with no one telling me what to do.

Sandra and I got our jobs back at the GEC, at last I am happy, a job I love and a good place to live. Sandra and I had lots of good times in the caravan; I still think of Bill and miss him.

Today at the bus stop on the way to work I met Dave, he is so nice we would get the bus to work most days, and I would look forward to coming home with him too. On Fridays and Saturdays we would go dancing at the club in town or go to the pictures, one day Sandra said I do not know Dave, something's not right you have not met his mum or dad, you do not know anything about him. I was just so happy with him having lots of fun.

Dave also had a caravan, on a Saturday I would stay at his van, but Sandra was right. Dave had a wife, she was having a baby and was with her mum, she was coming home soon, she had been very ill. I was very upset, how can he do that to his wife and me. That was it I did not want to see him again.

I cannot stay in the van anymore it is too upsetting, I have got a new job and a new home at the hospital in town, this time the matron will not be telling me what to do, I just hope I will be happy here. I love it on the wards, the patients are all so kind to me, I love to see them getting better and going home.

I have got some new friends, I met them at a rock and roll club, they became very good friends, Peter, Tony and Jeff. Over the years if I was sad or ill or anything they were there for me.

It is Saturday, it's my night off and I'm going dancing at a nightclub with the lads. Tony is very good at rock 'n roll, I love it too. A lad came and asked me to dance his name is John, he too can rock 'n roll. Tonight was so good I do hope I will see John again. The next Saturday at the club I met John, he is so good-looking we never stopped dancing all night, it was so good going out with him, we had lots of happy times, in time I met his mum and dad, I was very nervous, John had lots of aunts and uncles and one sister and brother they became my family, at the weekends I would stay with John and his mum and dad.

Christmas is coming and this time it will be so good to be part of a family, and be wanted and love Christmas Day.

It was the best ever, on Friday and Saturday nights John and I would go dancing at the club, we love rock 'n roll and also I would see the lads; they were always there for me. Tony has got a girlfriend she is very nice, and Peter too, we all met at the club on a Saturday night.

On Sundays John's aunts would come for dinner; Sundays for me had always been a bad day, everyone had gone home to their mum and dad's, now I have a family to go to.

I loved John's gran, she was so kind to me, I would go and see her when I was in town.

I had two very happy years with John, then I found out I was having a baby, and that was it, John and I fell out.

At the time I was still living at the hospital, I lost my job and had nowhere to live. I miss John and I missed John's family, but still go to his gran's. In time I found a bedsit to live in, all I had was a big bedroom and times were very hard, I was always in and out of hospital, I did think I was going to not have the baby but I did, and I love him. He was mine and no one was going to have him. His name is Brian, I took Brian to see Gran she was so happy, but I have not seen John or his mum and dad, but I'm very happy in my bed sit with just Brian and I, and Gran does not live far from me.

Today is not a good day I have cut my hand and got to go to the hospital it is very bad. I went to Gran's and she took Brian for me, but I've got to stay in hospital so Gran has asked John's mum to have him, so she had him at night and Gran during the day.

I miss Brian lots and wanted to go home, John came to see me today he said he misses me and loves me and wanted me back, then he gave me a ring and wanted us to get married, his mum came too and said you and Brian can come and live with us. I will look after Brian until your hand is better. So Brian and I went to live with John's mum and dad, it is good being in a house and not a bedsit. I am looking forward to the wedding, it will be soon, we have not got a lot, but that does not matter.

Today is my wedding day and I'm so happy. But I miss my dad.

John's family is now my family but I cannot call John's mum... Mum, or his dad... Dad. I never forget my dad, and no one can be my mum and so they are Jill and Jim. Nonetheless we all had a very happy day.

I am going to the hospital today with my hand it is not very good, it is my little finger the hospital want to cut it off. And at the hospital they asked me if I was having a baby. I did not know.

When I got home I said to John you're going to be a dad again, he was very happy.

John and I have got a house it is just across the road from his mum. This year has been very good, I have got married and have a house with John and Brian. I have never had a home that is all mine and now I'm having another baby.

It has been hard with John not being at work, his family are very good and they have Brian for me. It is coming up to Christmas and we will have the baby any day now, this time I will have a family and a home.

It is two days before Christmas and John has gone out with the lads Brian is in bed, I never did think that I could be so happy. But the baby is coming and John is still out. I had to go to his mum's; she cannot get John so she came to my house.

I have had a girl her name is Lisa, they will not let me come home for Christmas Day, but when I did come home on Boxing Day it was the best Christmas ever.

Don and Pat have come back to Stafford to live, it will be good for them to see Brian and Lisa, and they have two girls.

Today Don and Pat are coming to see me, I have missed them, Don and John do not get on, he has said John is not good for me, he is always out and comes home late.

I have got no food in the house and John is in the pub again, he is never in now and we fall out a lot, if it was not for his mum giving me food I do not know what we would do.

Today John is in the pub, his mum is out and I have not got any food again, I cannot do this anymore I'm going and taking Brian and Lisa with me.

I have not seen Sandra for a long time but that was where I went. She was so pleased to see Brian, Lisa and I, she took us all in. I did not want to go back, I was very unhappy I did think that John loved me, and I think I will always love him. But I think we got married too young, he was only 21, if I had not had Brian and then cut my hand, I do not think he would have married me but I had Lisa now too, and that was good, I love them both.

I could not stay with Sandra for long, and now I have got a house with my name on the rent book.

Now it's just me and the children, we do not have a lot. Don came to see us today with food and money, beds and everything for the house.

I was in town one day and met John, he said he misses me and can he come back. I said okay, but if we are not happy you will have to go because the house is mine.

It is the weekend and John is here, I just hope this time we will be happy. When I was living with John's mum, he met a girl, her name was Jo, she would bring John home from the pub, I always thanked her for looking after him, she was not happy at home she did not get on with her mum and dad, she stayed with us sometimes. One day when Jo was very upset she told me she was having a baby so I gave her a lot of Brian and Lisa's things.

Today John's mum, dad and gran are coming for tea, it is to say thank you for all that they did for me and the children.

I told John I am going to the shop and will not be long, when I got back Jo was there, and so was his family; John asked if I could see him in the kitchen, he said Jo had a fall out with her mum and has nowhere to go. It was not long for her to have her baby and I know it is not nice having no home so I said yes.

I was doing the tea when Gran came into the kitchen. Cindy I have got to tell you something, she said Jo is having John's baby, I am so sorry. Just then John came in, I was very upset. John is it true what Gran is telling me? He looked at me and said yes. What a fool I have been. She cannot stay here John said, and if she is going I have to go to, and with that they went.

I was very upset, but I still had his family. Brian and Lisa had a nan, gran, an aunt and uncle, a lot more than I had. I cannot stop them having a family; also they can see their dad.

Jo has had her baby, but she did not want it, he was adopted and his new mum and dad call him Jack, I never saw Jo again. John had lots of girlfriends; I was happy with Brian and Lisa. I have got to go to the hospital today with my hand, my neighbour is looking after Brian and Lisa, the doctor is saying I cannot put off having my little finger removed; it will never be any good.

The hospital, it is Standon Hall and I do not want to go. I did not think I would ever have to go back there again; during the operation John's mum is looking after Brian, and Don and Pat had Lisa, I was very nervous going back, but I was all right and everyone was very kind to me. I just wanted to go home to Brian and Lisa.

After that, times were hard I did not have a lot, it was just me and the two children; John would come round to see us, then when I had no money left he would go again.

But Tony and the lads were always there for me, Tony came on a Saturday we would all go into town or to the park, Tony would give me a bag of food if I had no money, the lads kept me going. In time Tony and Peter got married but they still came to see me we were all good friends.

One day Tony came, he was very upset he and his wife had fallen out, also John and I were apart, and the two of us were both very unhappy and the next thing we knew we were in bed. Tony was very sorry, but it was also me. After a week or two I went to the doctors, I was having a baby. I did not know what to do with Tony being married, and when John found out he too was not happy. But soon after he was okay, because he had a new girlfriend and was happy. His mum and dad said I was a bad mum, because I was having a baby and it was not John's, they wanted to take Brian and Lisa away from me, it was very hard, I did not know what to do, John's family did not want to know, only Gran was there for me, she was always there for me.

Tony had no mum and dad and was happy with his wife. It is coming up to Christmas and I will soon be having my baby, today Brian and Lisa have gone to their nan's, I am going into hospital to have my baby. Just me I hope I will be all right.

I had a girl, I called her Linda. Today Brian and Lisa came home, I have missed them lots, they loved Linda but their nan and all the family did not, they did not want to know, it was as if I had never had her. It was very hard for me, Linda only had me.

Just before Christmas John's family came to see Brian and Lisa with gifts and asked if they can have them for Christmas, I said no, they did not even look at Linda.

My three children and I had a good Christmas, one I will never forget. In the new year John's family came to see Brian and Lisa, but not Linda... they completely ignored her.

Tony came today; he was so upset that John's family were how they were. Tony was happy now and his wife did not know about Linda. Tony and his wife still came to see me, and Peter, but Tony's wife never did know that Linda was his, Tony came on his own too.

For weeks we did not know what to do, in the end we did think it best if Linda was with a new mum and dad, she only had me, I cannot take Brian and Lisa's family from them, all I can see is Brian and Lisa having a family if I pass away, and Linda having no one. With me being married to John he too was asked if Linda can have a new home, his mum and dad were not happy.

I did go and see Gran, she gave me lots of love and said she was sorry that Linda was going, but it was for the best, Linda would have a family to love her, I will never stop loving her and hope she will always be happy.

Tony came today to say goodbye, and to say he was sorry and that he will always be my friend and never forget me.

The next day John came, he stayed with me when they came and took Linda away. We were very upset, I will never forget that day. I just hope she will be loved and be happy.

The weeks have gone by and I miss Linda. John's mum has come to have Brian and Lisa for the weekend, she has never asked where Linda is, it is as if I have never had her.

I went into town today and met Tony, I was asking him if he knew anyone who can do some jobs for me at home, he suggested a man named Graham, and told me he will bring him to meet me at the house.

Tony came today with Graham, he is very nice. In time Graham was coming around a lot, he was very good with Brian and Lisa, and when the children were in bed he would come and see me. At weekends we would all go out in his car, he is very good to us. We now have food and the bills paid for, and it was all down to Graham. He looked after us all. If it was not for him I don't know how we would have got anything.

John did want to come back to me and sometimes he did, but it never did last and he was gone, but Graham was always there for me.

In time Graham said it was John or him; it was Graham and I will never see John again. And after eight years we got married, we did not have a lot when we got married. I got a job and we got a new home, I am very happy, Brian and Lisa are happy too. Graham is very good to them.

Graham got a caravan and we all went to the seaside, we had lots of happy times in the caravan.

Today I am very nervous; I have got a new job at a hospital in the kitchen, and looking after the patients. I love it, I have got new friends one was Norma, and she too had had a very unhappy time when she was growing up, she can understand me on the days I am not happy, remembering the things Mary did to me, her dad was not good to her.

I was always at work weekends and at night, with it being a hospital, Christmas too. Norma was always with me. These were very happy years, we had happy times in the caravan, and I also had good Christmases with Graham and Brian and Lisa Graham's mum, dad and sister were also good to me.

Don came to see me today, he told me Mary is very ill, she wants to see me to put things right, I was very nervous, I did not go and the next day she passed away.

I did not go to the funeral I was away, I went to the doctors I was remembering all that she did to me, I had forgotten; I cannot do this, I wish it will all go away. I go to the doctors every week and tell him what I remember, it is very hard, Graham was very loving and understanding. I also had Norma and at this time Brian and Lisa had left school. Brian went into the army at 16, I did not see him a lot after that and Lisa went to the hospital, she is good at looking after everyone.

Don came today, he said we have to go and see if I want anything of Mary's, there are photos of Dad you can have, Mary had left the house and got a flat. So I went, everything was in boxes, but I soon found photos of Dad, there was one of Dad that I had had in my school bag, it was taken from me when I went in the home all those years ago and now I have got it back.

I also found a picture Dad had given me a long time ago, "Don look at this" it fell apart and in the back was a wedding picture, Don just looked at me, he said "this is Mum and Dad."

It was our mum and dad, and that was why Dad asked me to look after the picture, it was what was inside it.

Back home I was so happy, I had never seen a photo of my mum, Don said I look just like her.

In time I did not have to go to the doctors anymore.

I am a lot happier now, I do have bad days when I remember, but she cannot hurt me anymore. I have Graham he is a good man, Norma and other good friends and Brian and Lisa are doing very well and happy.

Today I have got a new job at the GEC, I worked there a long time ago, no more weekends or nights and Christmas at home.

I was very nervous, but soon I love it, things were never the same after that. I did a lot of happy things. Penny, Denise, Tracy, Bill and Linda; Bill was the boss originally, and when he left Penny became my boss. I had never travelled far away, but soon I was going to London for the weekend with them all from work, and going out down the town, they all became very good friends. Brian worked down the factory he too became a good friend.

Down the factory they had a club and went away for a long weekend every year, I went too. The first time I went across the channel to France I was very nervous I had never left the UK before, I had a fantastic time, we also went at Christmas to Holland and Germany, Bruges, Lille and Normandy. Graham came too, I had lots of very happy times.

At home Graham and I kept fish, we would go at the weekends to aquarium shops, over the years we had lots of happy times.

Today I am very sad, my best friend has passed away, I will miss her lots, it will not be the same going away without her. We had very happy times in France and Holland.

Graham has always wanted to go to the Maldives to see the fish, so down town today I have booked for us to go for a holiday; we have never been on a plane before. At work they

are so very happy for us, and we have had lots of gifts to tak
with us.

Today is my birthday; I had a good time at work Penny mad
me a cake, we all have lots of fun at work.

At last the day has come for us to go on holiday to the Maldives
we are so excited, it was a long time on the plane, but at last we
are here we just want to go to bed. The next day when we go
out it was so hot we went in the sea; it is not far from our room
We had a fantastic time, but all too soon it was time to go home
we took lots of photos I will never forget that holiday. Back at
work they wanted to know all about it and look at the photos.

Years went by and I am very happy, Penny Denise and Brian
are still my very good friends.

This year I am going to retire from work, I will be 60.
Today is my last day at work, I am sad and happy. I will miss
them all, they were very happy times and of course I will still see
them, and go away, they will always be part of my life.

I'm going to the Stafford Crown Court to see Carolyn for an
interview to be a volunteer, I am very nervous, but I got the
position, I have got to do some training, so I can do the
paperwork and look after the witnesses. A child under the age of
18 is very vulnerable, when they give their evidence it is by a
live-link, I went for a week's training to look after children from 2
- 18 years and also a week's training to look after all witnesses.
One of the volunteers is Daphne and she is a very good friend.

Today is not a good day Graham is not well, he is in pain I
asked him if he is all right, he wasn't so I had to ring for an
ambulance, he had had a heart attack, he was very ill over the
next four years, it was hard. He was in and out of hospital all the
time, he will never get better. Graham had two heart attacks.

Daphne was always there for me; and Penny and Denise, also
down the factory was Tom, he became a good friend.

For a long time now I have been thinking of going to the County Council for my records, to find out about my childhood.

Today is the day I will get my records from the council, Daphne is going with me. I found out a lot of things from my records it is a lot to take in. I will never forget that day, the lady said we would be there for about an hour, but we came out three hours later. I was so pleased that Daphne was with me, there was a lot to look at, I hope one day I can understand all that is in my records.

I was led to believe that I was placed into care at a very young age, the truth is that is not so. I did have a mum and dad who loved me lots. Mum was in and out of hospital but Dad was there to look after me and my brothers when Mum was very ill, before she passed away we went to foster parents, which were two doors away, so Dad was always coming around to see us. I was almost three, it was true that we were all evicted and put into care; it will be a long time for me to take in what is in my records, a lot I do not remember it is very upsetting.

I was always in a world that was happy, a happy home and someone to love me so remembering the truth was very hard, I have lots of good friends and Graham, without them I do not think I can do this, it is so hard, also Don and Pat were good to me too, they came to see me and I look forward to their letters. When I look back I was never told the truth, and I was always in my world not the real one.

The last forty years have been very happy I have Graham and lots of good friends, Lisa and Brian who I love, and happy times to look back on, weekends away or just going out to town to see Penny or Denise and remembering the happy times at work.
I was in town today and met a lady, she asked me if I was Don's sister, and that she went to school with me, we were soon remembering lots of happy times with my dad.

She was going to a birthday party and asked me if I would come too, and meet up with the girls I went to school with. I said yes. I had a very happy night, it was so good to see them all again Don came too. When Don was telling me about our stepmother having a baby, I did not think of Dad at the time, I do now, he must have been very upset she was his baby too and my sister. If she had lived I do think would we all have been happier?

I was asking him about my records, he did not want to say, then he was telling me all about our stepmother when she married Dad, she was having a baby, then just before Geoff and I came home she lost it. She took it out on me, she did not want to bring me home, it was all right if Dad was around, but when he was at work she was not nice. Two years later she had a girl, but sadly she only had her for one day. I do not remember, but Don said after that it was a very sad time.

The next five years we did have happy times, we all went to the seaside for two weeks. I also went to Clent to see Gran and Aunt Olive, I love it there, Aunt Olive had a son his name was Graham, we had fun days looking after the horses and going with Gran to clean the school. I have not seen Graham for a long time I don't know what happened to him.

I was always at the railway station to see Dad, we also had happy Christmases too, Dad had three days off.

Then when Dad got killed on the railway our stepmother took it very hard, and again it was me she took it out on. It must have been very hard for Mary when Dad got killed on the railway I do know that she loved him, when we went away for a holiday I did hope that it was going to be all right, we did have a good time and she was okay, when we got home she took it out on me again big time.

I do understand her now after all these years, but I cannot forgive her I just wanted to be loved and wanted. I am 70 now and very happy, and I thank all my friends, Graham, Lisa and Brian.

I would not be here now if it was not for them.

Many years have gone by, but I have never forgotten Linda, I think of her most days and hope she is happy and loved, one day I hope to find her, and tell her that I have never stopped loving her, and tell her all about her family. I know I will never be her mum; I just want her to be happy. And tell her that me and her dad were very good friends until the day he passed away, she was never forgotten, we did think of her often.

I still see Don, he is eighty now, and we remember the happy times we had with Dad and Mary, I do not see Geoff very much. I will never forget you Dad and I still miss not having a mum, I did not have a happy beginning but I am very happy now, thanks to all my friends and Graham and my family.

(not) The End...

Printed in Great Britain
by Amazon